HOW TO STOCK
YOUR
FIRST KITCHEN

A GUIDE OF WHAT TO BUY,
HOW & WHERE TO STORE IT,
& USE AND CARE PRINCIPLES

By MARY FISHER KNOTT

HOW TO STOCK YOUR FIRST KITCHEN

(a guide of what to buy, where & how to store it, and use & care principles)

By
MARY FISHER KNOTT

Published by: **KNOTT COMMUNICATIONS**
Post Office Box 3755
Alhambra, Ca., 91803, U.S.A.

Copyright © 1984 by Mary Fisher Knott
First edition
Printed in the United States of America
Library of Congress No. 83-90390
ISBN 0-911701-00-1

ABOUT THE AUTHOR

Mary Fisher Knott is an author, lecturer, and teacher of kitchen design; and since graduation from college, has designed over 4,500 kitchens for her clients. She recently finished a national media tour where she appeared on many television talk shows, was interviewed by newspaper editors and radio commentators about her approach to organizational design and management of kitchens. From the many letters and questions she received from people all over the country, she has written this book, addressing the challenge faced by those trying to stock, outfit, and organize a kitchen with basics for the first time.

Mary is the author of other kitchen and home decorating guides:

BRIDE & GROOM'S DECORATING FILE
(a guide in decorating and organizing an apartment or condominium)

KITCHEN REMODELING FILE
(a file folder with instructional guides and check lists designed to organize your kitchen remodeling project and kitchen plan: covering everything involved from how to measure your kitchen to lighting, appliance, floors, and storage)

222 KITCHEN PLANS
(222 kitchen floor plans and elevations)

CONTENTS

INTRODUCTION

"If You Have The Proper Tools, You Can Do The Job Right"

For years, my Dad stressed to me the importance of doing a job right and having pride in a job well done. The difference between doing something right and just doing something is having the skill to do the job and having the correct tools with which to do the task. This is quite evident in my field, that of kitchen design. We all have seen the work of craftsmen and in contrast that of workmen who just get by. Having the proper tools and the skill to use them makes the difference.

When it comes to outfitting a kitchen, this principle is also true. Select the best quality utensil your budget allows you to buy, learn how to use it, and care for it properly.

All of us have favorite recipes which require specific tools or utensils to prepare them; make sure these tools or utensils are included on your shopping list. (i.e., my food processor is certainly not essential to start a kitchen, but I would hate to be without it.)

When shopping for your basics, there are many price options at your disposal. Supermarkets, hardware and department stores, discount stores and gourmet-speciality shops have inventory to meet your needs; their prices and quality will vary.

Remember this guide is a foundation on which to build a well-equipped kitchen and as you begin to develop your skills in food preparation, and develop recipes, you will want to add to your stock of tools and utensils.

BASIC COOKING UTENSILS

BASIC COOKING UTENSILS

Listed in this shopping list are utensils basic for preparation of a variety of menus; so consider the type of meals you plan on preparing in your kitchen to determine the tools you'll need. For example, a bride furnishing her first kitchen will want all the equipment listed so she can prepare a variety of menus. On the other hand, a bachelor or bachelorette concerned with limited meal preparation, such as fresh vegetables and meat and weekend breakfast, may want to delay the purchase of baking equipment.

KITCHEN
TOOLS &
COOKWARE

FOOD PREPARATION TOOLS

VEGETABLE PEELER

METAL TONGS

4-SIDED GRATER

LARGE STRAINER

VEG. BRUSH

WOODEN SPOON

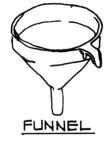
FUNNEL

WIDE RUBBER
SPATULA

NARROW RUBBER
SPATULA

COLANDER

2 - PASTRY
BRUSH

KITCHEN FORK

LG. PANCAKE
TURNER

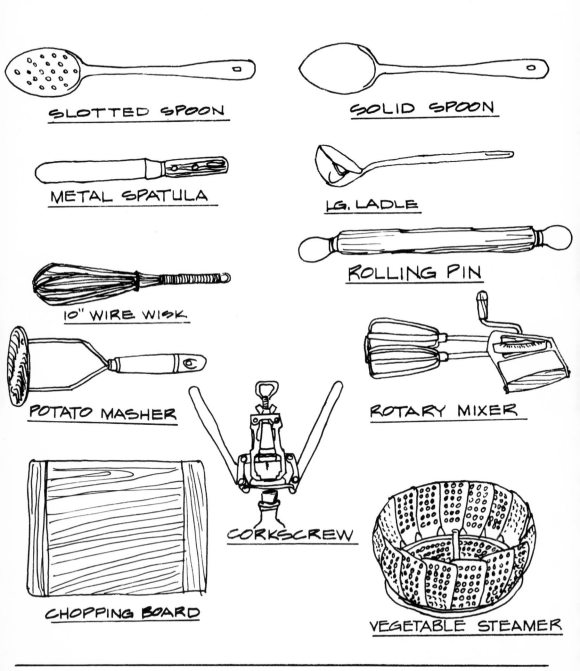

SLOTTED SPOON

SOLID SPOON

METAL SPATULA

LG. LADLE

10" WIRE WISK

ROLLING PIN

POTATO MASHER

ROTARY MIXER

CHOPPING BOARD

CORKSCREW

VEGETABLE STEAMER

MIXING & MEASURING UTENSILS

1 SET - MIXING BOWLS

MEASURING
CUPS

MEASURING
SPOONS

PITCHER

BAKING EQUIPMENT

BREAD PAN

2- BAKING SHEETS

2 ROUND CAKE PANS

9" PIE PAN

SQUARE CAKE PAN

2QT. CASSEROLE
w/ COVER

2 WIRE CAKE RACKS

1½ QT. CASSEROLE
w/ COVER

KNIVES

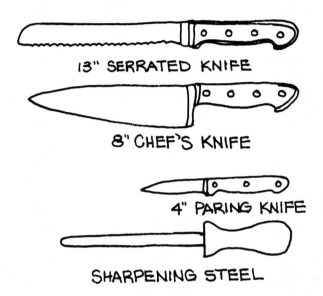

13" SERRATED KNIFE

8" CHEF'S KNIFE

4" PARING KNIFE

SHARPENING STEEL

FOOD STORAGE & FREEZING

PLASTIC
CONTAINERS

LARGE
& SMALL JARS

POTS & PANS

8" SKILLET w/LID

IQT. SAUCE PAN
(w/LID)

12" SKILLET (w/LID)

3QT. SAUCE PAN
(w/LID)

ROASTING PAN
w/RACK TO FIT

SMALL PAN
w/LID

KITCHEN LINENS

HAND & DISH TOWELS

POT HOLDERS & MITS

DISH CLOTH & SPONGE

SMALL APPLIANCES

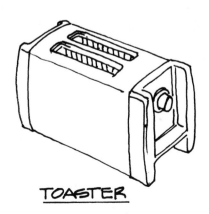

TOASTER

COFFEE MAKER

TABLE SERVICE

 PLATE

 BOWL

 CUP & SAUCER

 PLATTER

 VEG. BOWL

 BUTTER DISH

 SALT & PEPPER

 SUGAR & CREAMER

 FLATWARE

 2 TRAYS

 JUICE

 TUMBLER

 WINE GLASS

 SERVING FORK

 SLOTTED

 SOLID SERVING SPOONS

BASIC RULES FOR STORAGE

BASIC RULES FOR STORAGE

This storage guide will help you organize your kitchen taking advantage of available cabinet and storage space. Storage accessory items currently on the market will help extend the space you have; try to include them (as your budget allows) in your kitchen. Following are some of the most useful ones: roll-out shelves for base cabinets, wall racks, drawer dividers, racks which attach to cabinet doors, narrow rack and shelves for the back of counters, wooden knife holders (especially those with an angle).

Courtesy: Mary Fisher Kitchens

REMEMBER: THE BEST STORAGE TOOL YOU HAVE IS THE PERIODIC INSPECTION AND DISCARDING OF UNUSED, UNNECESSARY ITEMS.

Note: Decorate with many of your utensils and tableware items. They are then stored and add to the room at the same time. Baskets are my favorite storage accessory. (Terrific for some fruits and vegetables).

STORAGE AREAS

For utensils, equipment, supplies, and food. Store in each center the supplies and utensils to be used there. When an item is used in more than one center, store it in the place of the first use. The following list of locations to store various items (from the Cornell University Study) may also be used as an inventory list.

Courtesy: Mary Fisher Kitchens

STORAGE AREAS

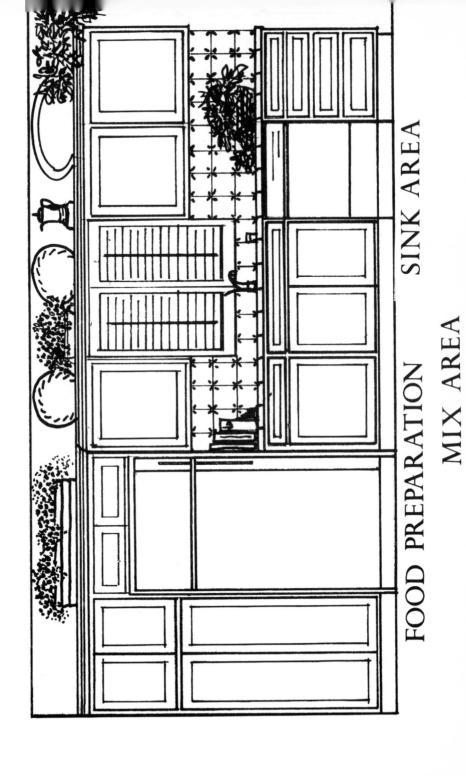

SINK AREA

MIX AREA

FOOD PREPARATION

STORAGE AREAS

SERVE RANGE AREA

FOOD PREP./MIXING

LOCATED BETWEEN SINK
& REFRIGERATOR
WHEN REFRIGERTOR OR
OTHER WALL, MIXING &
FOOD PREPARATION CENTERS
ON COUNTERS AT THE SINK

SINK/CLEAN UP

LOCATED AT SINK & DISHWASHER
INVOLVES FOOD PREPARATION,
CLEAN UP, & DISH STORAGE

RANGE/SERVE

AREA SURROUNDING THE
RANGE OR COOKTOP
INCORPORATES COOKING
& SERVING OF FOOD

WHERE TO PUT WHAT

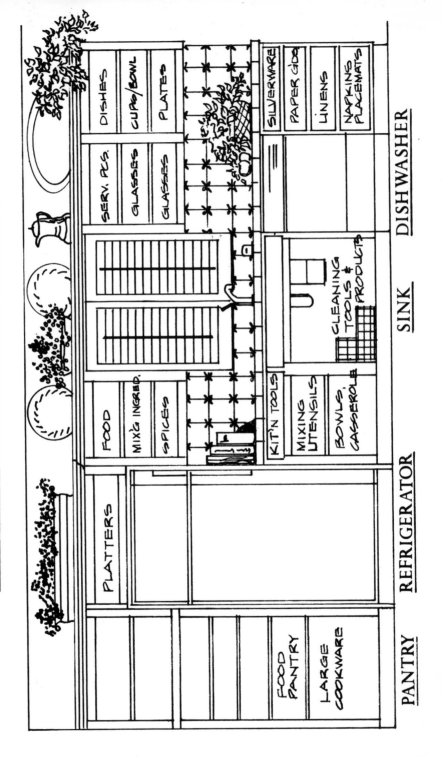

PANTRY   REFRIGERATOR   SINK   DISHWASHER

BASIC RULES FOR GENERAL FOOD STORAGE

Unpack groceries promptly. Wrap meats, fish, poultry, and other foods in air-tight packages or place in air-tight containers for the freezer. (I like to label and date freezer items at this time. Use masking tape and a black felt-tip pen). If you have to keep food frozen in an emergency, wrap it in several layers of newpaper. Transfer the contents of opened cans into covered glass jars or refrigerator containers. Baskets make great containers for storing items like onions, potatoes, oranges and other foods needing cool, dark, vented areas. Cut off extra leaves but do not prepare vegetables until ready to use. Storing nuts, dried fruit, coffee, bread and cereals in air tight containers in the refrigerator adds to the life of those foods. (Coffee, nuts, breads and pastries freeze successfully for long periods of time).

Courtesy: Mary Fisher Kitchens

STORAGE RULES (cont.)

FRESH VEGTABLES

Wash, drain and store in the crisper,
allowing room for some air circulation.
Store lettuce, celery and carrots in
sealed plastic bags in the refrigerator.
keep watercress, leaves down, in a
bowl of cold water in the refrigerator.
Wrap asparagus in wet kitchen towels
or paper towels and store in
refigerator.

STORAGE RULES (cont.)

FRESH FRUITS

Bananas should be stored at room temperature. (Putting them in the refrigerator darkens them). Berries and other fruit should be stored on a flat tray. **DO NOT WASH** until ready to use. Avocados, pears, pineapples, melons, bananas, and tomatoes continue to ripen at room temperature. (When ripe, store in refrigerator).

HERBS, SPICES, LEAVENINGS

Keep herbs and spices in a cool, dark place. (Not above the range). Date herbs and spices when purchased. They loose their potency after a year has past and should be discarded, keep leavening agents in refrigerator; except for dry yeast, it may be stored in a cool, dry, place.

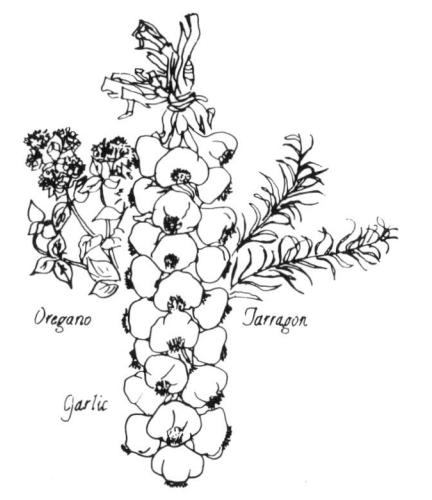

Oregano   Tarragon

Garlic

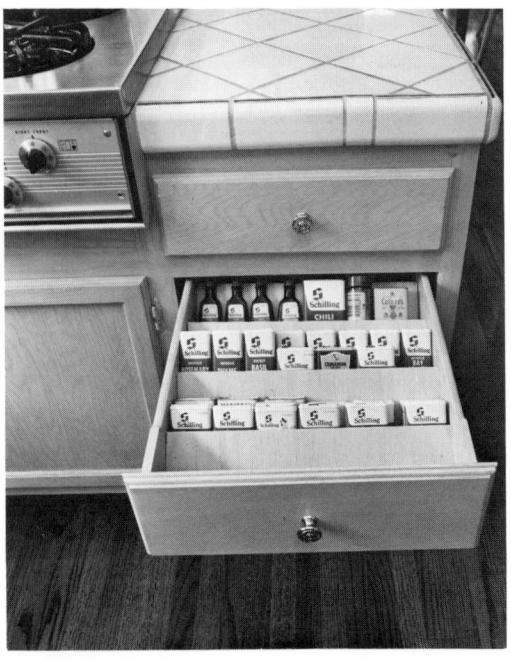

Courtesy: Mary Fisher Kitchens

STORAGE RULES (cont.)

MILK AND EGGS

Keep milk covered, in refrigerator. Cover cooked foods containing milk, cool quickly and use soon. Store eggs, small end down in the refrigerator. Do not wash until you're ready to use them.

BUTTER & CHEESE

Butter & margarine take on flavors so be sure to cover for storage.
Cheese should be stored in air-tight, moisture-proof bags in the refrigerator.

STORAGE RULES (cont.)

POULTRY

Wrap in freezer paper for freezing or in plastic wrap or waxed paper for the refrigerator. Poultry keeps for about 4 days in the refrigerator.

MEAT

Unwrap fresh meat; place in the refrigerator, either put on the rack in your meat container or lay on a plate; top lined with waxed paper. DO NOT WASH. Prepare within 2 days. Freeze all meat if storing longer than 2 days. Cut or divide meat into desired servings before freezing. Cover cooked meat stored in the refrigerator.

FISH

Frozen fish should be wrapped heavily while in the freezer. Fresh fish to be served within 24 hours should be wrapped lightly and stored as you do fresh meat.

STORAGE RULES (cont.

STAPLES

Dried foods, nuts: Keep dried fruits in sealed packages or jars in cool, dry areas. Dried peas, beans and nuts should be in air-tight containers. If there is room, keep peanut butter, cheese spreads, and candied fruits in the refrigerator.

Cereal Grains: Store flour, corn meal, oatmeal, breakfast foods in a cool place, (not over the refrigerator). For long storage, use covered, air-tight containers and put in the refrigerator. (As you may have gathered by now, the refrigerator is one of your most useful, money-saving items in the kitchen; buy the best and largest you can afford and that fits into your kitchen).

Syrups, Liquid Honey: Store honey, covered, at room temperature to prevent crystallation. (If it does crystallize, place the jar in warm water.) Store syrups in a cool place.

Cookies & Crackers: Store in containers with tightly fitting lids. Do not combine crisp and soft cookies or sweet cookies and crackers.

STORAGE RULES (cont.)

FATS. OILS, & SHORTENINGS

Oils & Shortening can be stored in cool areas for limited periods of time. (6 months) Fats, Oil & Shortenings which have been used but not heated to smokey may be reused and must be stored in the refrigerator in a covered container.

KITCHEN STORAGE NOTES

Courtesy: Armstrong Co.

Taking advantage of all available space inside and out of cabinets, is a key to achieving the best storage system possible in your kitchen. In this section of the book, we will be looking at some specific kitchens and how additional storage space was created by using cabinet accessories and some design variations. The kitchens featured consist of apartment and condominium units.

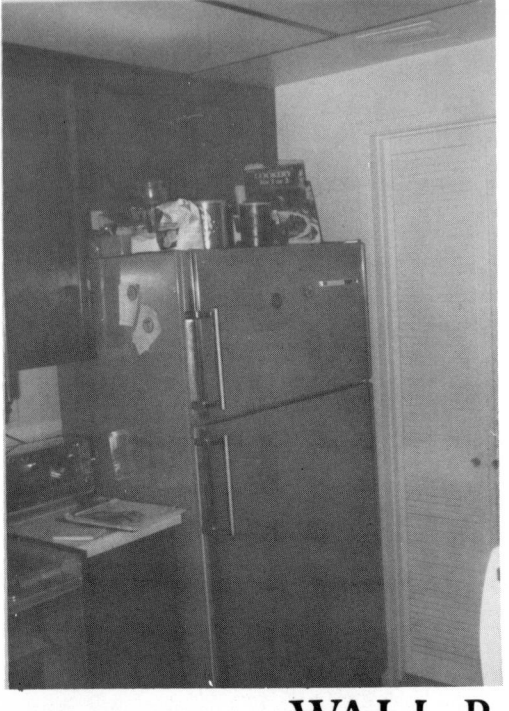

WALL B

WALL A

↳EXISTING PANTRY

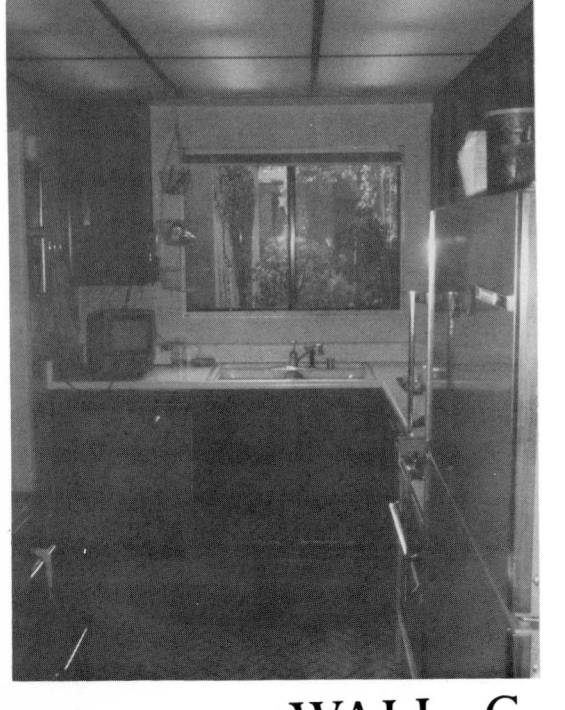

CREATING MORE STORAGE
SPACE CAN BE ACHIEVED
BY ADDING CABINET STORAGE
ACCESSORIES & REDESIGNING
WALL A TO INCORPORATE
NEEDED COUNTER SPACE,
STORAGE & EATING SPACE.

FRESH PAINT, WALLCOVERING,
& LIGHTING WILL ENLIVEN
THE KITCHEN & MAKE IT
SEEM BRIGHT & AIRY.

WALL C

KITCHEN A

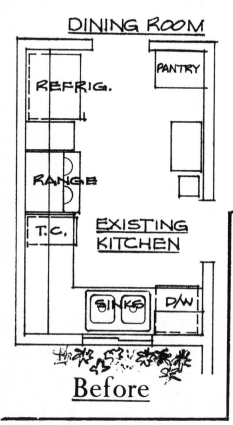

DINING ROOM

REFRIG.

PANTRY

RANGE

T.C.

EXISTING KITCHEN

SINKS D/W

Before

PROBLEM AREAS:

- .INADEQUATE STORAGE
- .NEED MORE COUNTER
- .NEED EATING SPACE
- .POOR LIGHTING

SOLUTIONS:

- .ADD STORAGE TO WALL A
- .ADD COUNTER TO WALL A
- .ADD PULL-OUT EATING COUNTER
- .ADD UNDERCABINET LIGHTING

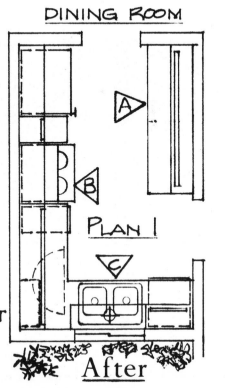

DINING ROOM

PLAN 1

After

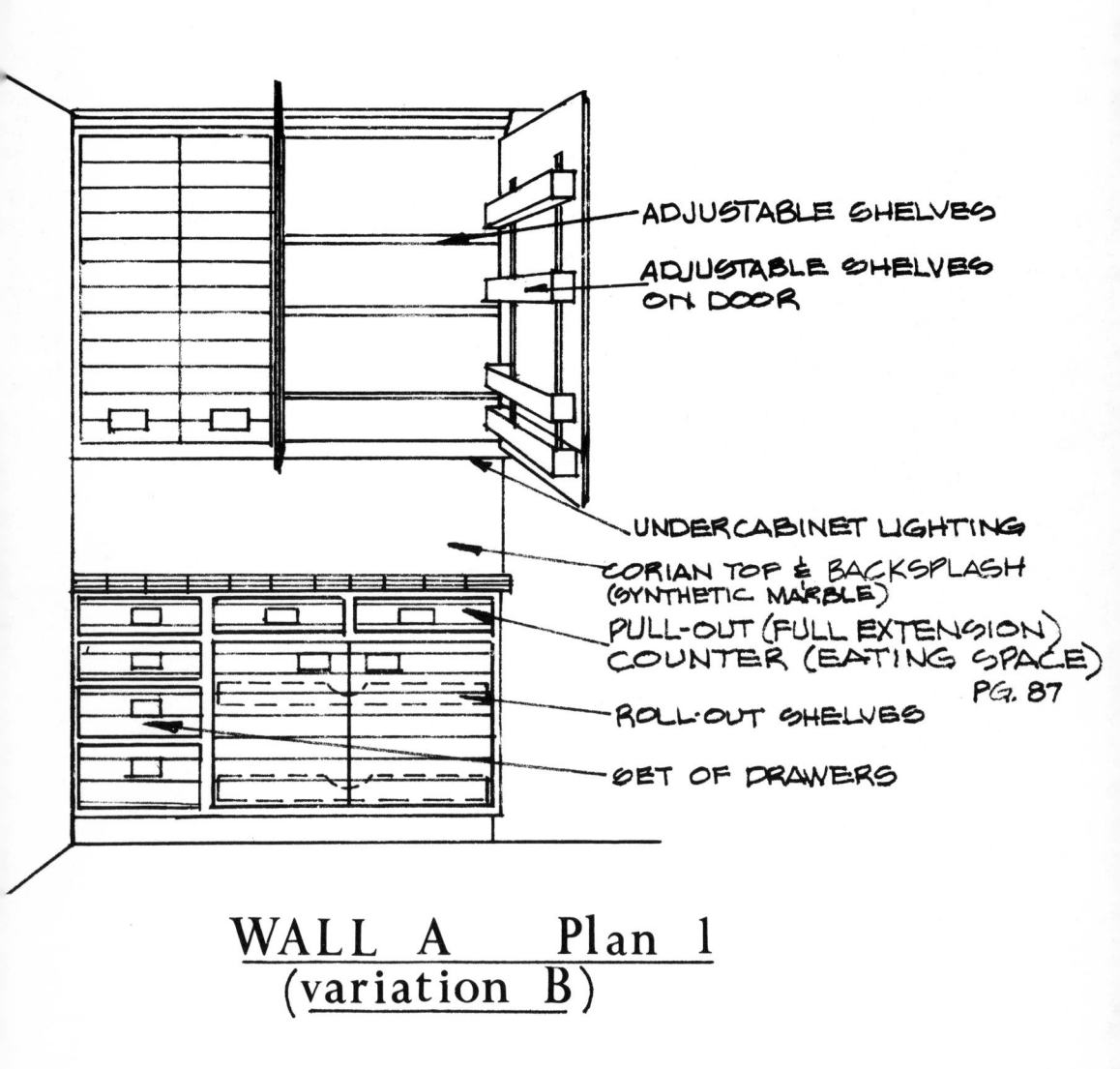

ADJUSTABLE SHELVES

ADJUSTABLE SHELVES ON DOOR

UNDERCABINET LIGHTING

CORIAN TOP & BACKSPLASH (SYNTHETIC MARBLE)

PULL-OUT (FULL EXTENSION) COUNTER (EATING SPACE) PG. 87

ROLL-OUT SHELVES

SET OF DRAWERS

WALL A   Plan 1
(variation B)

NOTES

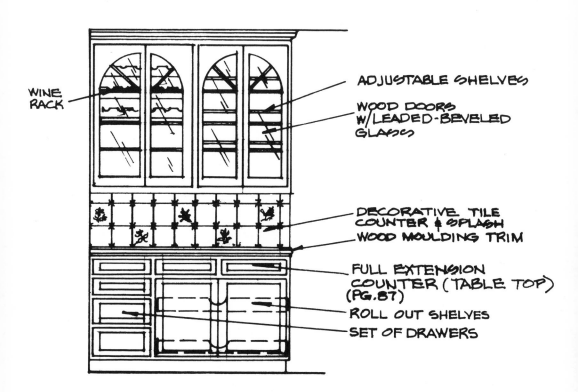

WINE
RACK

ADJUSTABLE SHELVES

WOOD DOORS
W/LEADED-BEVELED
GLASSES

DECORATIVE TILE
COUNTER & SPLASH
WOOD MOULDING TRIM

FULL EXTENSION
COUNTER (TABLE TOP)
(PG.87)
ROLL OUT SHELVES
SET OF DRAWERS

WALL A   Plan 1

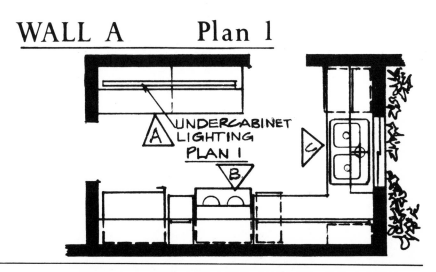

UNDERCABINET
LIGHTING
PLAN 1

A

B

C

NOTES

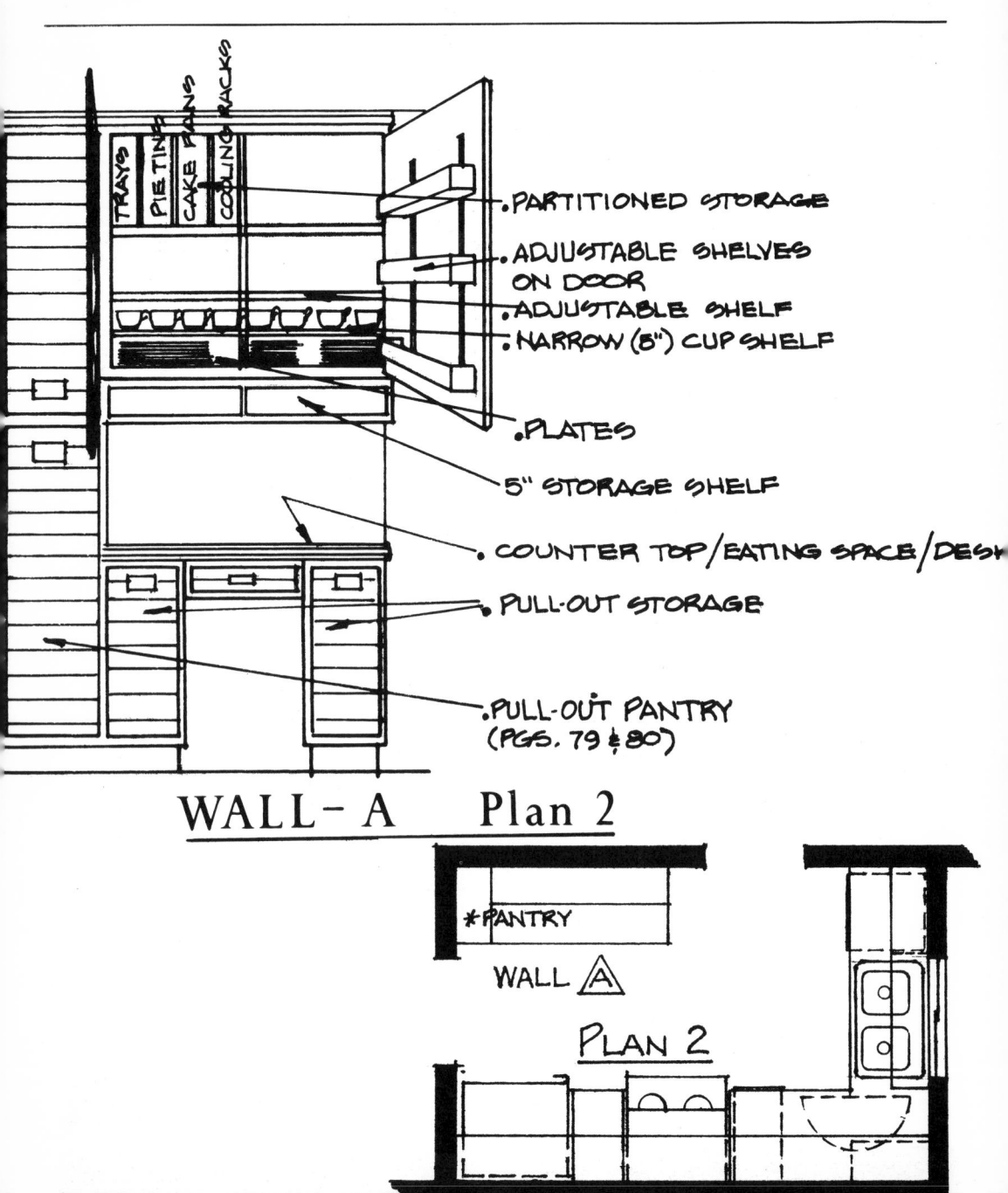

TRAYS

PIE TINS

CAKE PANS

COOLING RACKS

- PARTITIONED STORAGE
- ADJUSTABLE SHELVES ON DOOR
- ADJUSTABLE SHELF
- NARROW (5") CUP SHELF
- PLATES

5" STORAGE SHELF

- COUNTER TOP/EATING SPACE/DESK
- PULL-OUT STORAGE

- PULL-OUT PANTRY (PGS. 79 & 80)

WALL - A   Plan 2

*PANTRY

WALL Ⓐ

PLAN 2

NOTES

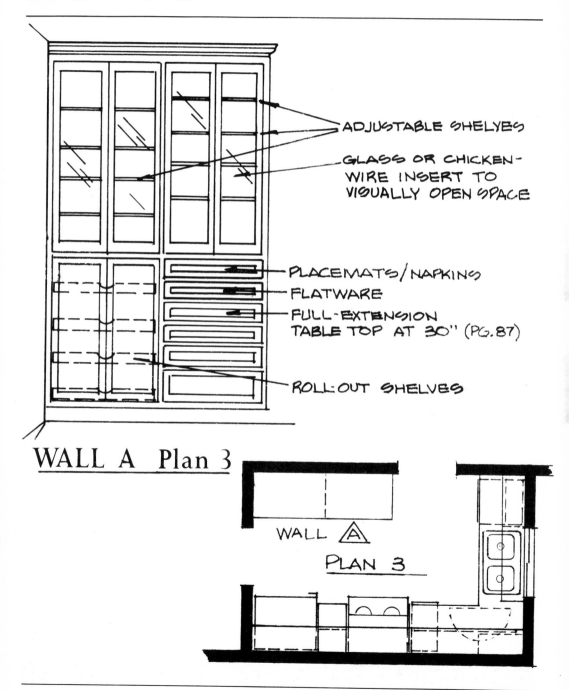

ADJUSTABLE SHELVES

GLASS OR CHICKEN-
WIRE INSERT TO
VISUALLY OPEN SPACE

PLACEMATS/NAPKINS

FLATWARE

FULL-EXTENSION
TABLE TOP AT 30" (PG.87)

ROLL-OUT SHELVES

WALL A Plan 3

WALL Ⓐ

PLAN 3

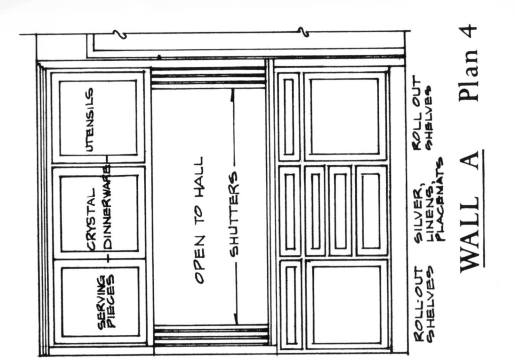

UTENSILS

CRYSTAL · DINNERWARE

SERVING PIECES

OPEN TO HALL

SHUTTERS

ROLL OUT SHELVES

SILVER, LINENS, PLACEMATS

ROLL-OUT SHELVES

WALL A   Plan 4

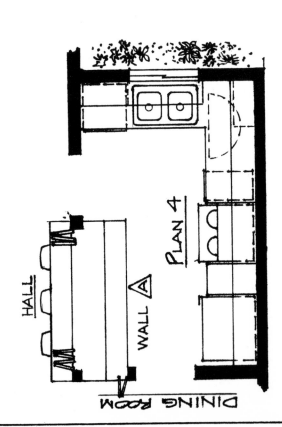

HALL

WALL A

PLAN 4

DINING ROOM

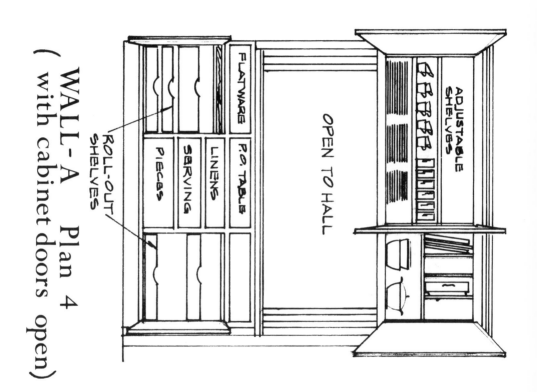

ROLL-OUT SHELVES

FLATWARE

P.O. TABLE

LINENS

SERVING

PIECES

OPEN TO HALL

ADJUSTABLE SHELVES

WALL - A   Plan 4
(with cabinet doors open)

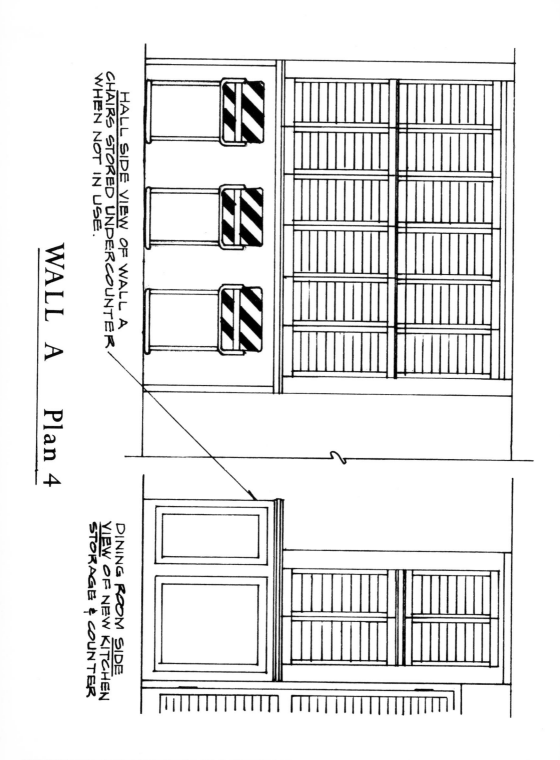

HALL SIDE VIEW OF WALL A
CHAIRS STORED UNDERCOUNTER
WHEN NOT IN USE.

DINING ROOM SIDE
VIEW OF NEW KITCHEN
STORAGE & COUNTER

WALL A   Plan 4

53

NOTES

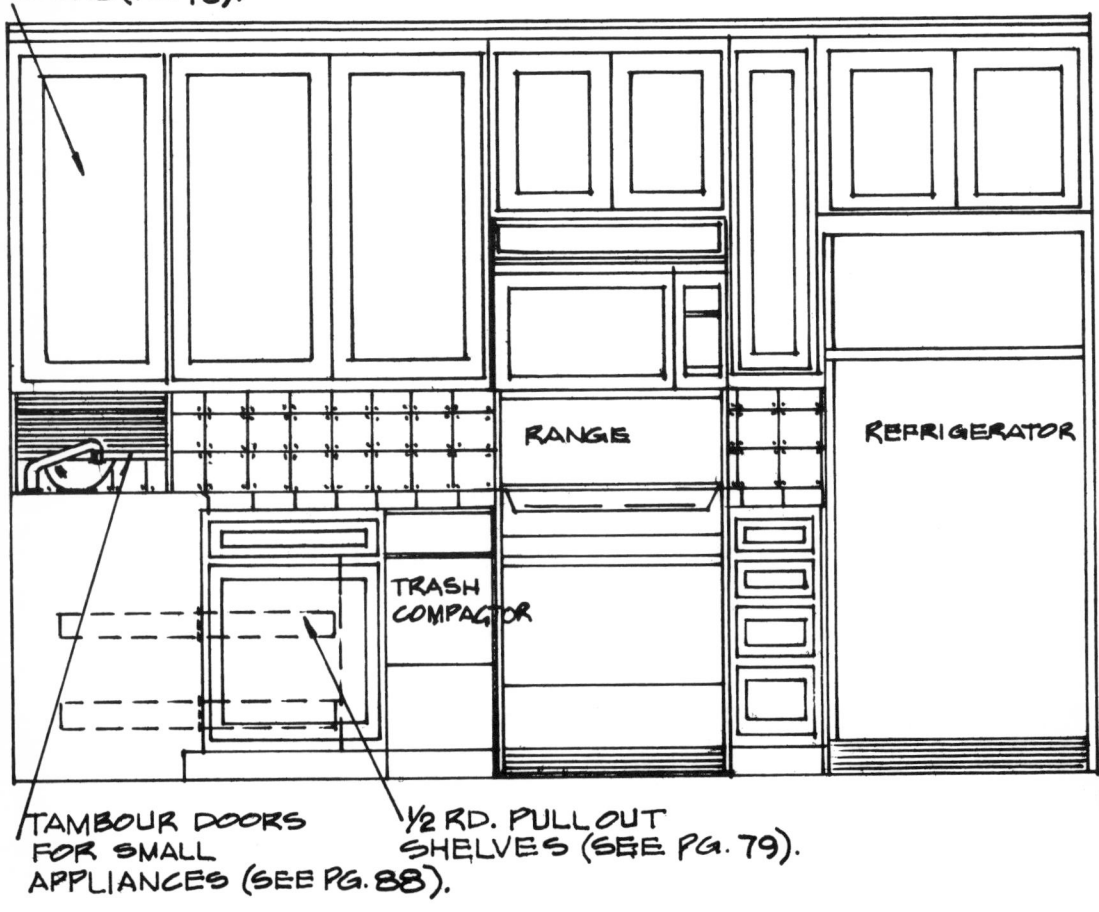

ADD ½ SHELVES & STORAGE ON DOORS (PG. 75).

RANGE

REFRIGERATOR

TRASH COMPACTOR

TAMBOUR DOORS FOR SMALL APPLIANCES (SEE PG. 88).

½ RD. PULL OUT SHELVES (SEE PG. 79).

WALL - B

NOTES

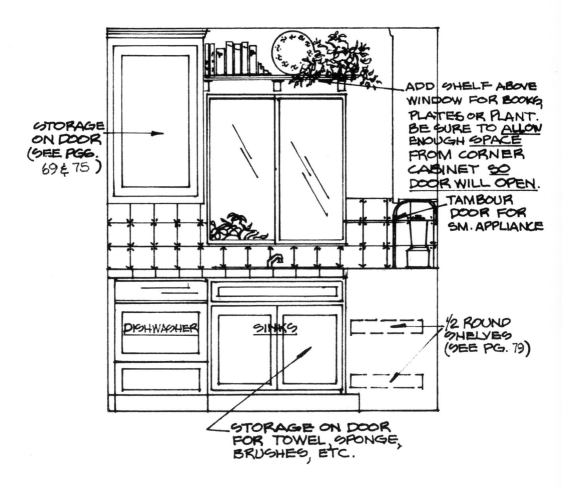

STORAGE ON DOOR (SEE PGS. 69 & 75)

ADD SHELF ABOVE WINDOW FOR BOOKS, PLATES OR PLANT. BE SURE TO <u>ALLOW</u> ENOUGH <u>SPACE</u> FROM CORNER CABINET <u>SO</u> DOOR WILL OPEN.

TAMBOUR DOOR FOR SM. APPLIANCE

DISHWASHER

SINKS

½ ROUND SHELVES (SEE PG. 79)

STORAGE ON DOOR FOR TOWEL, SPONGE, BRUSHES, ETC.

WALL - C

KITCHEN B

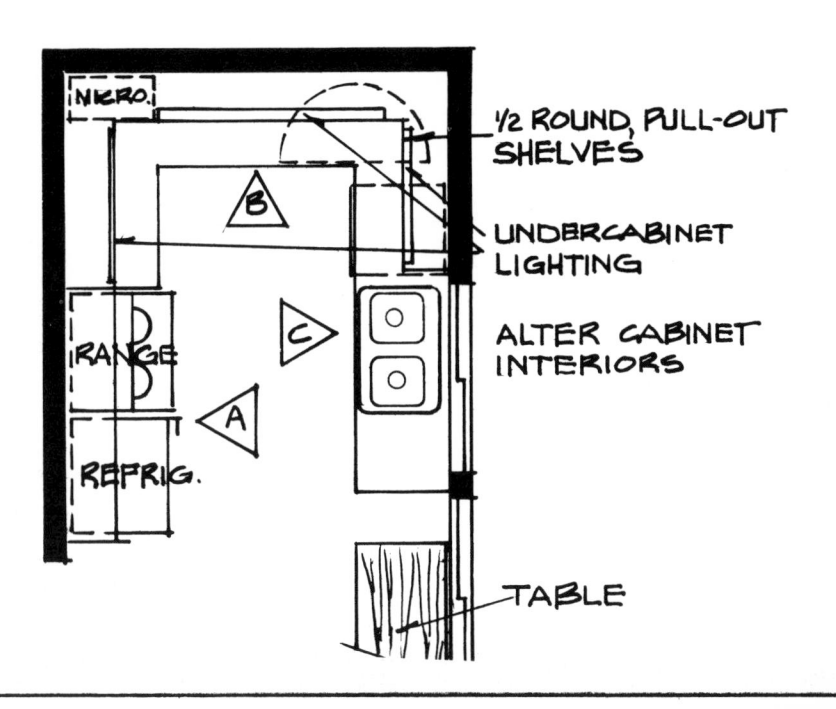

½ ROUND, PULL-OUT SHELVES

UNDERCABINET LIGHTING

ALTER CABINET INTERIORS

TABLE

NOTES

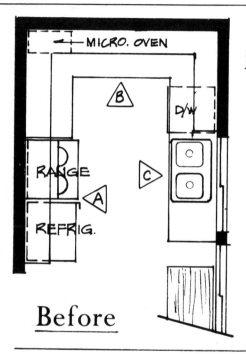

Before

PROBLEM AREAS:

- INADEQUATE STORAGE
- POOR LIGHTING
- STORAGE IS HARD TO REACH

SOLUTIONS:

- ½ ROUND, PULL-OUT SHELVES
- UNDERCABINET LIGHTING
- ALTER CABINET INTERIORS

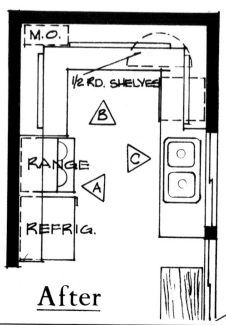

After

WALL B

AFTER

NEW SHELVES

NEW SHELVES

BEFORE

NOTES

NOTES

Base Cabinet — WALL B

BY ADDING ½ ROUND, FULL EXTENSION SHELVES TO BASE CABINET YOU'LL GAIN EASY ACCESS TO CORNER SPACE.

½ ROUND, FULL EXTENSION SHELVES (SEE PAGE 79)

NOTES

KITCHEN B

FRENCH BREAD RACK ADDS STORAGE FOR TV & BOOKS

NOTES

A FRENCH BREAD RACK
PROVIDES STORAGE
FOR COOKBOOKS, T.V.,
INDOOR PLANTS.

WINDOWS ARE TREATED
WITH SHUTTERS & PAINTED
WHITE TO MATCH WALLS

THIS MAKES THE ROOM
SEEM LIGHT & AIRY.

KITCHEN C

A NEW HUTCH GIVES STORAGE & COUNTER SPACE.

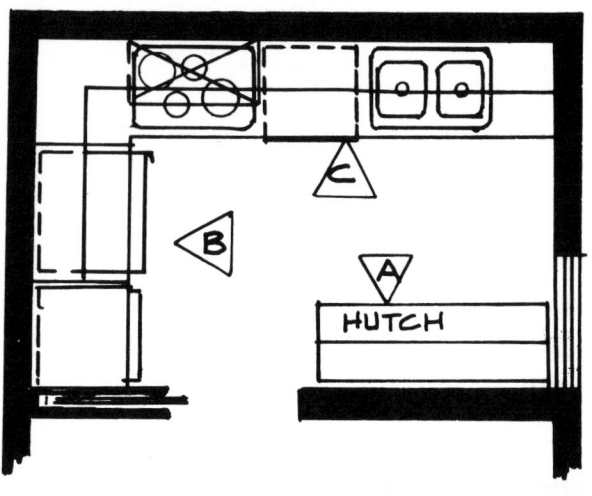

NOTES

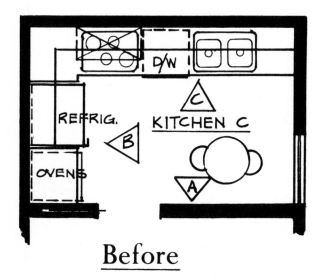

PROBLEM AREAS:

- INADEQUATE STORAGE
- POOR LIGHTING
- INADEQUATE WORK SPACE
- TOO MANY APPLIANCES

Before

SOLUTIONS:

- ADD NEW CABINET ON WALL A
- REORGANIZE EXISTING CABINETS
- ADD UNDERCABINET LIGHTING

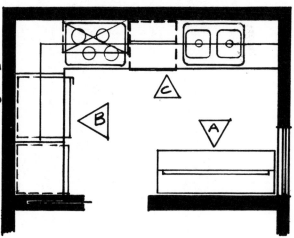

After

NOTES

BEFORE

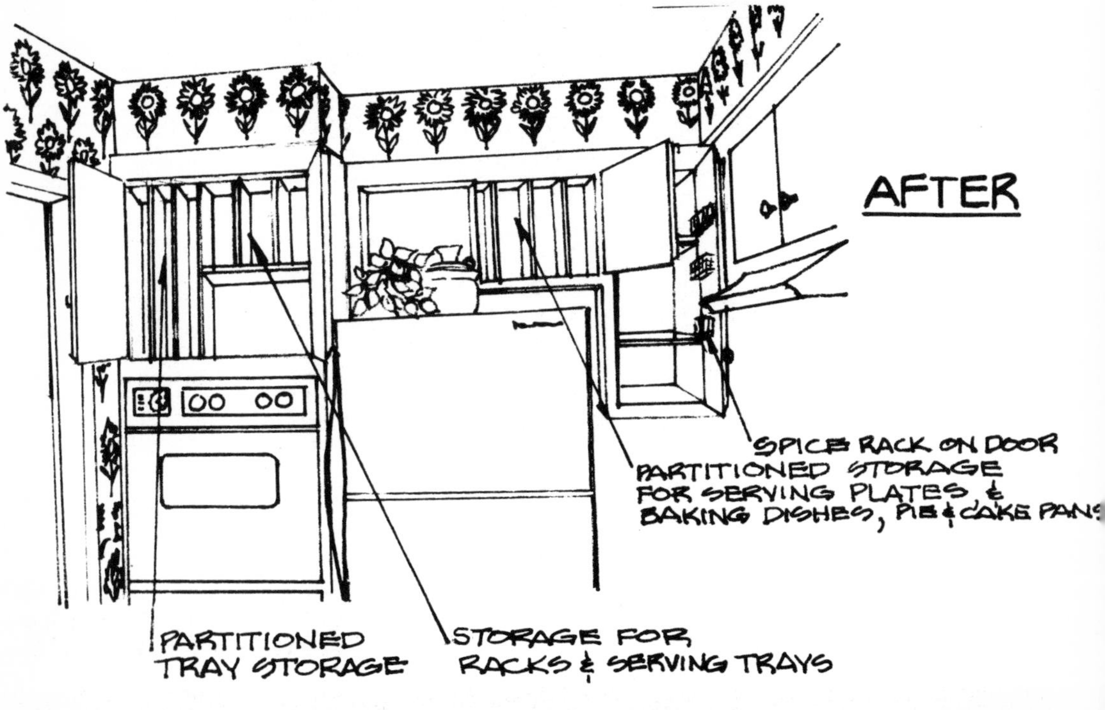

AFTER

SPICE RACK ON DOOR
PARTITIONED STORAGE
FOR SERVING PLATES &
BAKING DISHES, PIE & CAKE PANS

PARTITIONED
TRAY STORAGE

STORAGE FOR
RACKS & SERVING TRAYS

NOTES

<u>BEFORE</u>

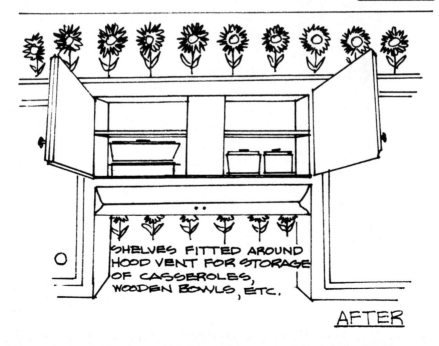

SHELVES FITTED AROUND HOOD VENT FOR STORAGE OF CASSEROLES, WOODEN BOWLS, ETC.

<u>AFTER</u>

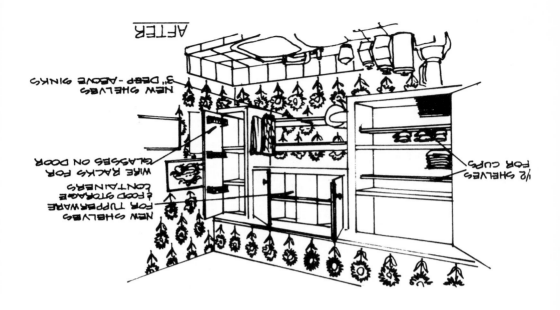

AFTER

NEW SHELVES
3" DEEP - ABOVE SINKS

WIRE RACKS FOR
GLASSES ON DOOR

NEW SHELVES
FOR TUPPERWARE
& FOOD STORAGE
CONTAINERS

1/2 SHELVES
FOR CUPS

BEFORE

NOTES

NOTES

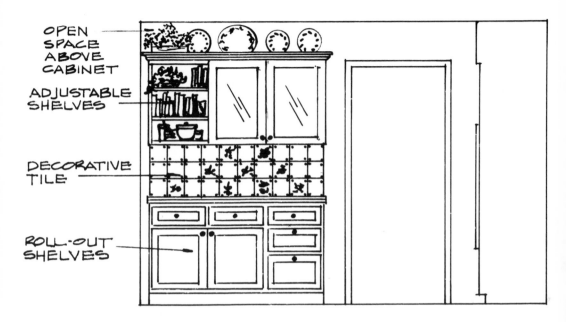

OPEN SPACE ABOVE CABINET

ADJUSTABLE SHELVES

DECORATIVE TILE

ROLL-OUT SHELVES

WALL - A   STORAGE

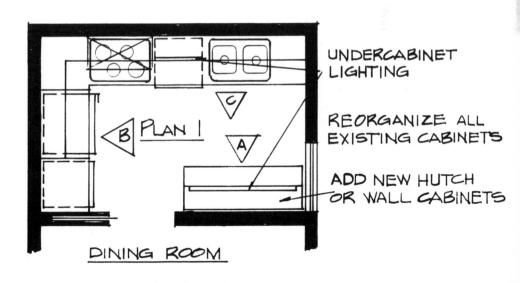

UNDERCABINET LIGHTING

REORGANIZE ALL EXISTING CABINETS

ADD NEW HUTCH OR WALL CABINETS

B   PLAN I   C   A

DINING ROOM

NOTES

STORAGE UNITS

TODAY, THERE ARE LITERALLY HUNDREDS OF CABINET STORAGE ACCESSORIES ON THE MARKET. THEY CAN EXTEND YOUR STORAGE SPACE BY 30-40%.

WE HAVE, IN THE FOLLOWING PAGES, SELECTED SOME OF THEM TO SHOW YOU SELECTION & APPLICATIONS. SHOULD YOU WISH INFORMATION ON SIZES, COST OR AVAILABILITY, CONTACT ME % KNOTT COMMUN. CO., P.O. BOX 3755, ALHAMBRA, CALIFORNIA, 91803.

WIRE BASKETS FOR
MOUNTING ON CABINET
DOORS.

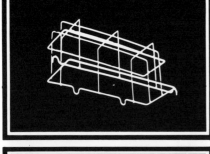

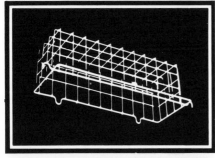

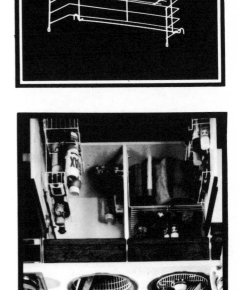

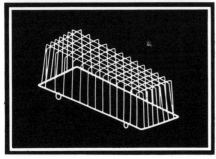

NOTES

NOTES

BY ADDING A SHELF UNIT TO THE DOOR & SHELVES INSIDE THE CABINET, THIS BROOM CLOSET CONVERTS TO A NICE PANTRY, & UTILITY STORAGE CABINET.

PHOTOS OF STORAGE ACCESSORIES COURTESY OF:
- AMEROCK
- ELFA
- HÄFELE
- POGGENPOHL

NOTES

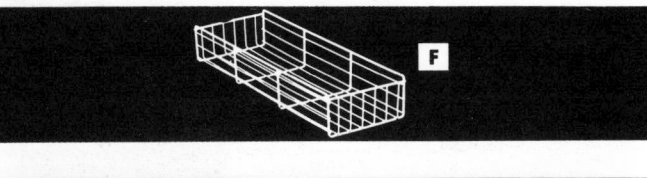

E - SM. WIRE BASKET
J - LID RACK
K - RAG BASKET

F - MED. WIRE BASKET

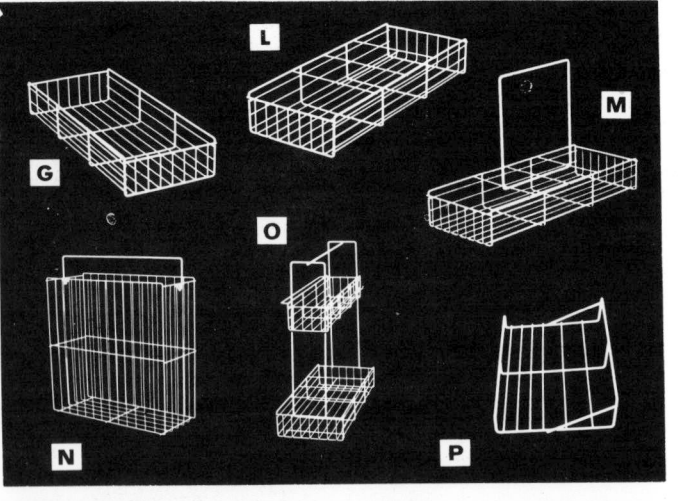

G - LG. WIRE BASKET
L - BOTTLE BASKET
M - BOTTLE BASKET
    W/ HANDLE
N - LAUNDRY BASKET
    W/ HANDLE
O - BASKET FOR
    CLEANING PRODUCTS
P - SHOE SHELF

H - LG. WIRE TRAY
Q - WINE BOTTLE SHELF
R - LG. SHOE SHELF

NOTES

A

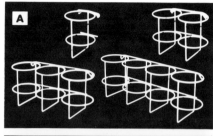

A

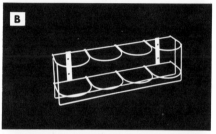

B

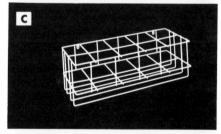

C

C

D

D

BOTTLE HOLDERS

NOTES

THE WELL THOUGHT
OUT ORGANIZATION
OF THESE OVERHEAD
CABINETS SHOW
EFFECTIVE USE
OF SPACE.

ALTHOUGH THIS
CABINET SPACE IS
ORGANIZED, THE
CENTER STYLE
SHOULD BE RE-
MOVED FOR EASIER
ACCESS TO SPACE.
(THIS WILL MEAN
 NEW CABINET
 DOORS).

NOTES

ADDING STORAGE RACKS TO CABINET
DOORS INCREASES USABLE STORAGE.
(BE SURE DOOR HINGES WILL CARRY
THE WEIGHT OF ITEMS TO BE STORED).

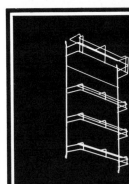

Measurements: Width x Depth x Height

Depth

Width

Height

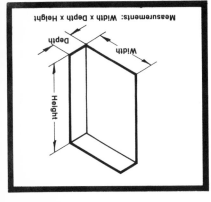

B

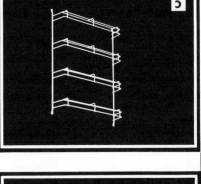

E

D

C

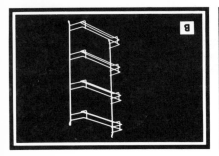

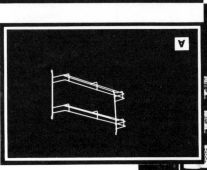

A

SPICE STORAGE RACKS

NOTES

NOTES

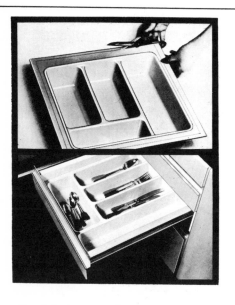

TRAYS FOR FLATWARE & UTENSILS
CAN BE CUT TO SIZE TO FIT
INTO AN APPROPRIATE DRAWER

A MAGNETIC RAIL MOUNTED
ON WALL OR SECURED IN A
DRAWER WILL HOLD KNIVES
OR UTENSILS SECURELY IN
PLACE.

JAR OPENER MOUNTED ABOVE
COUNTER MAKES OPENING
JARS EASY.

NOTES

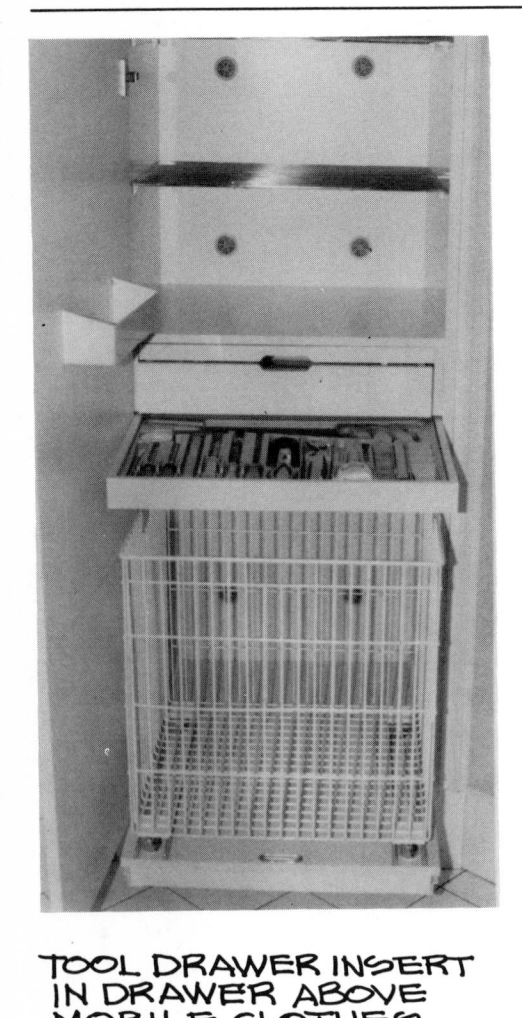 

TOOL DRAWER INSERT
IN DRAWER ABOVE
MOBILE CLOTHES
HAMPER.

HANDLED BASKETS,
(CAN BE REMOVED),
HOOKS & TOWEL BAR
PROVIDE ADDED STORAGE

TAKE A 24" WIDE CLOSET, CABINET OR WALL
SPACE & MAKE A USEFUL ALL-PURPOSE
STORAGE CABINET.

NOTES

STATIONERY ½ SHELF ADDED FOR STORAGE OF SMALLER CONTAINERS.

OAK SPICE SHELF IS USED FOR STORAGE OF SMALL CANNED GOODS, LEAVING SPACE TO THE LEFT FOR TALLER ITEMS. WIRE BASKET ON DOOR FOR LIGHT-WEIGHT STAPLES.

WIRE BASKET WITH TOWEL ROD & BRUSH HOOKS HAS BEEN ADDED TO SINK CABINET DOOR.

NOTES

CONVERT NARROW SPACES TO USEFUL STORAGE CABINETS WITH PULL-OUT SYSTEMS.

BELOW:
½ ROUND, FULL EXTENSION SHELVES PROVIDE EASY ACCESS TO CORNER CABINETS.

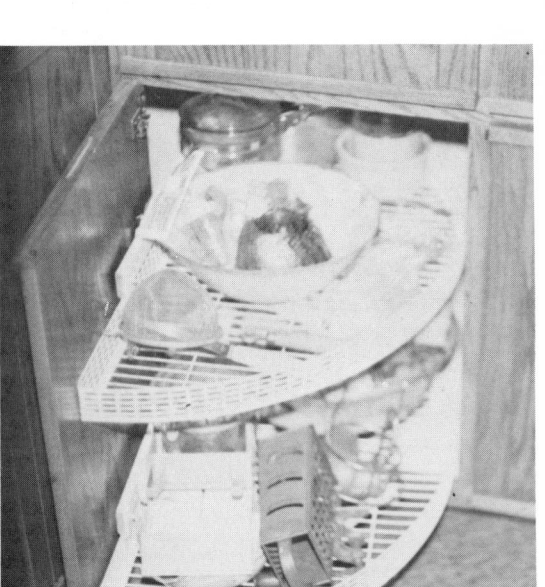

NOTES

PULL OUT PANTRY

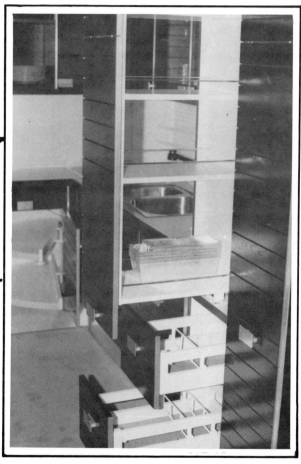

NOTE ½ ROUND SHELVES FOR EASY ACCESS TO BASE CORNER CABINETS

NARROW, 24" DEEP, TALL SPACES MAY BE EFFICIENTLY USED BY INSTALLING PULL OUT STORAGE UNITS.

NOTES

STORAGE
SPACE
ABOVE

KITCHEN SCOOPS FOR
DRY INGREDIENTS.

KITCHEN
SCOOPS FOR
TALL SPACE

PAPER GOODS STORED ON
UPPER CABINET DOOR.

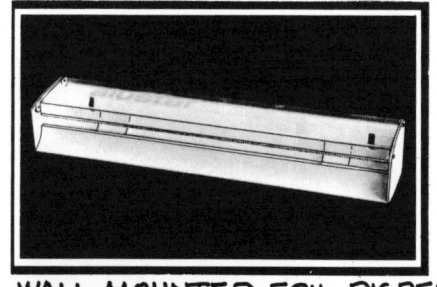

WALL MOUNTED FOIL DISPENSER

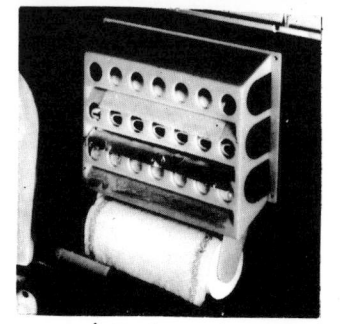

FOIL & PAPER DISPENSER.

NOTES

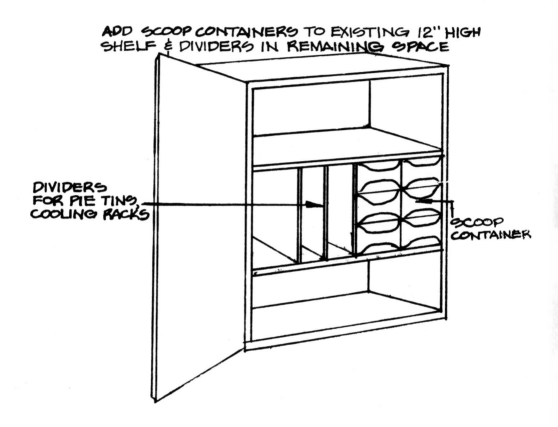

ADD SCOOP CONTAINERS TO EXISTING 12" HIGH
SHELF & DIVIDERS IN REMAINING SPACE

DIVIDERS
FOR PIE TINS
COOLING RACKS

SCOOP
CONTAINER

NOTES

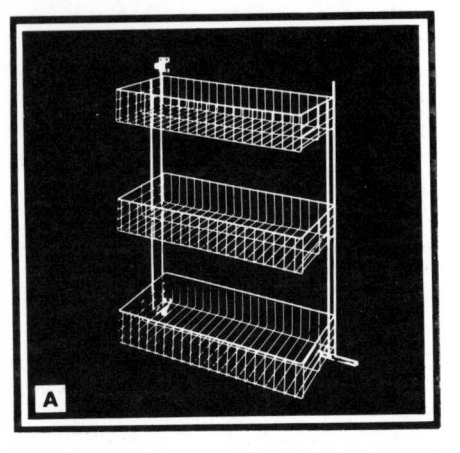

A

STORAGE CABINET SHELF

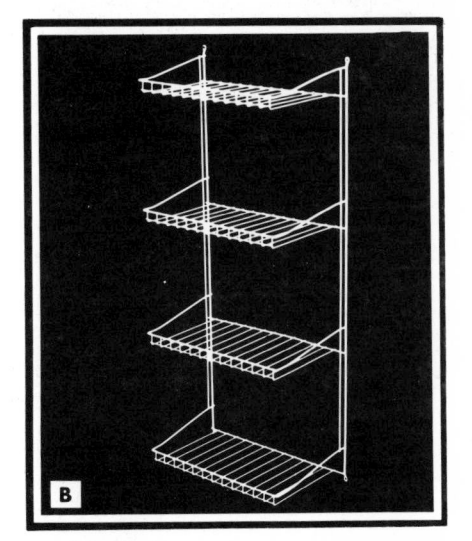

B

BROOM CLOSET SHELF

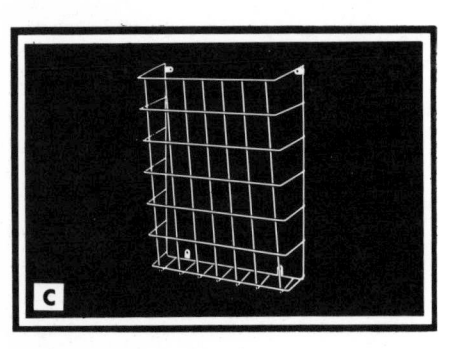

C

RAG BASKET

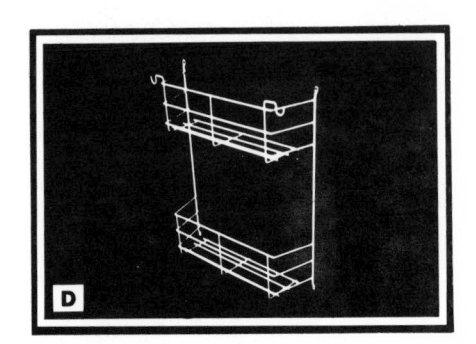

D

UTENSIL HOLDER

NOTES

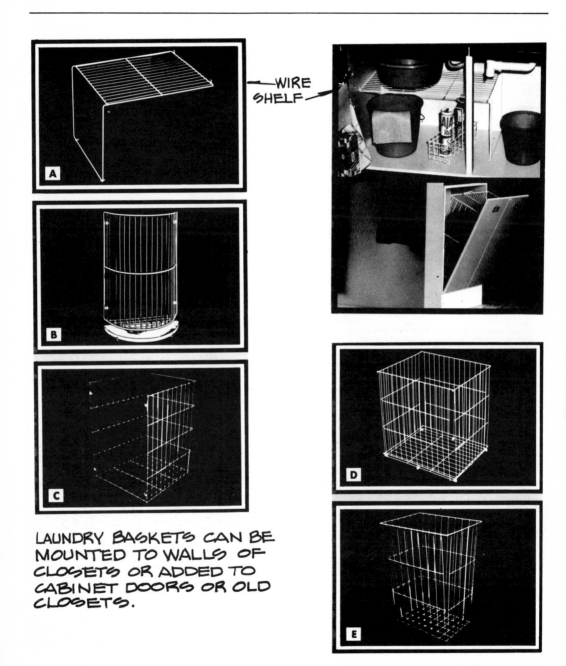

WIRE SHELF

A

B

C

D

E

LAUNDRY BASKETS CAN BE
MOUNTED TO WALLS OF
CLOSETS OR ADDED TO
CABINET DOORS OR OLD
CLOSETS.

NOTES

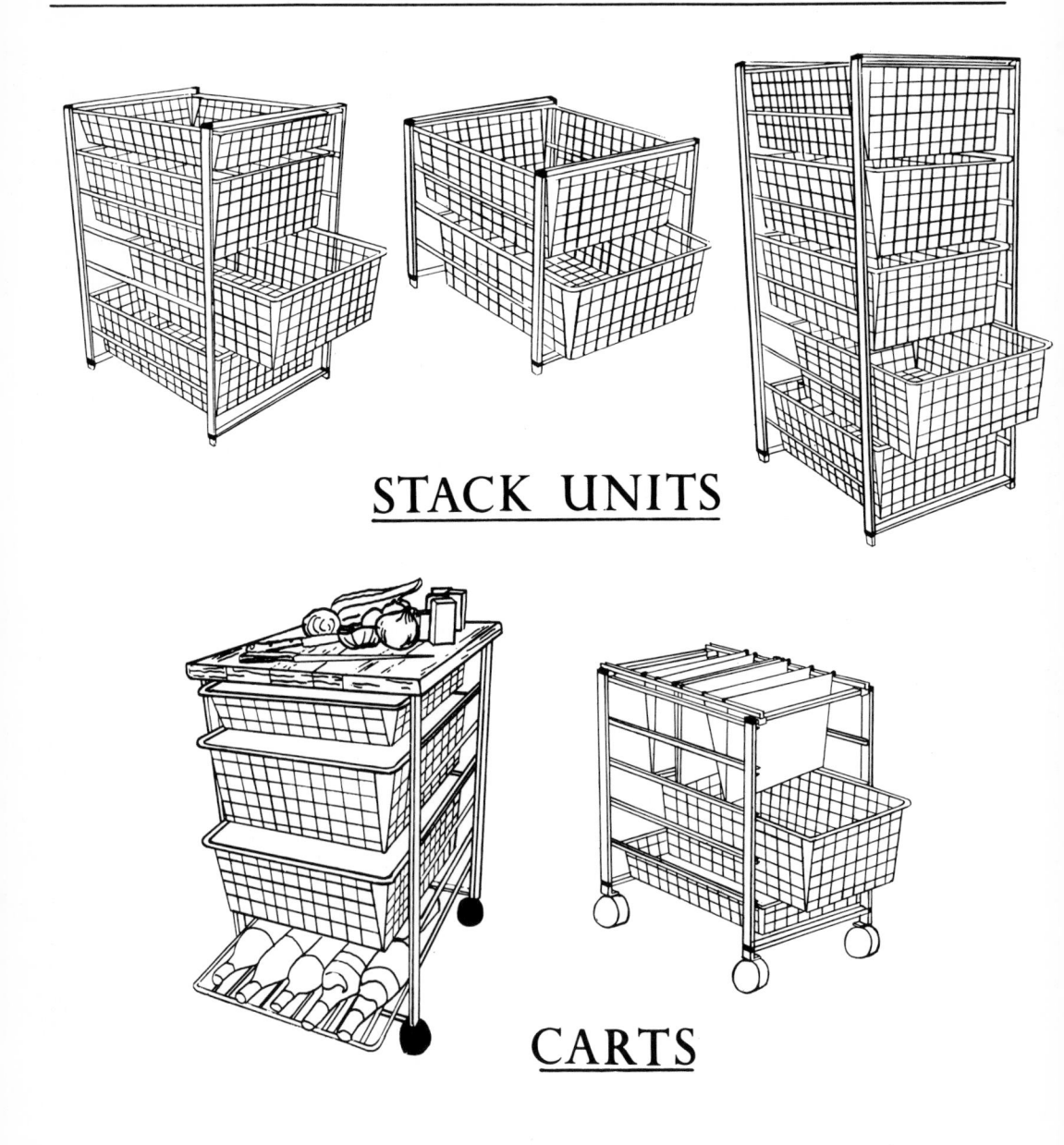

STACK UNITS

CARTS

NOTES

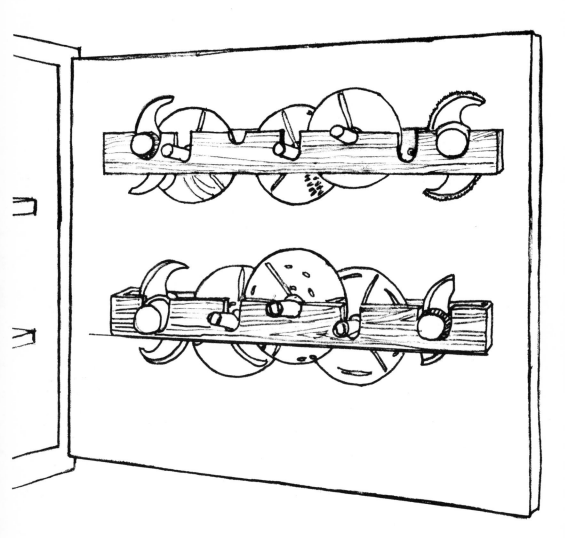

FOOD PROCESSOR BLADE RACK
(INSTALL IN MIX AREA—NEAR PROCESSOR)

NOTES

A FULL EXTENSION TABLE
MAY REPLACE A DRAWER
AND PROVIDE YOU MUCH
NEEDED EATING & WORK SPACE.

A POP-UP SHELF FOR HEAVY,
SMALL APPLIANCES CAN BE
ADDED TO A CABINET SPACE.

NOTES

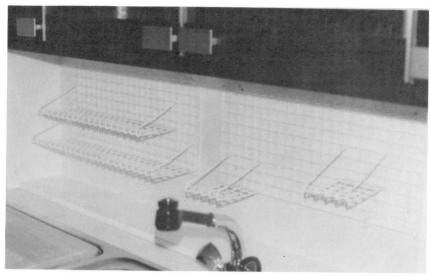

WIRE GRIDS & SHELVES PROVIDE USE OF WALL
SPACE BETWEEN COUNTER & CABINET.

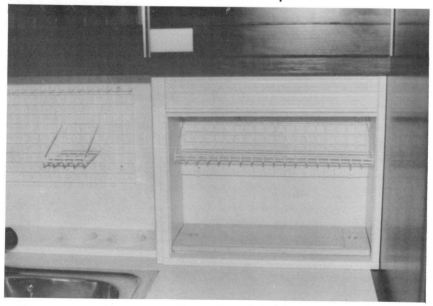

TAMBOUR (ROLL TOP) DOOR
CAN PROVIDE HIDDEN STORAGE.

NOTES

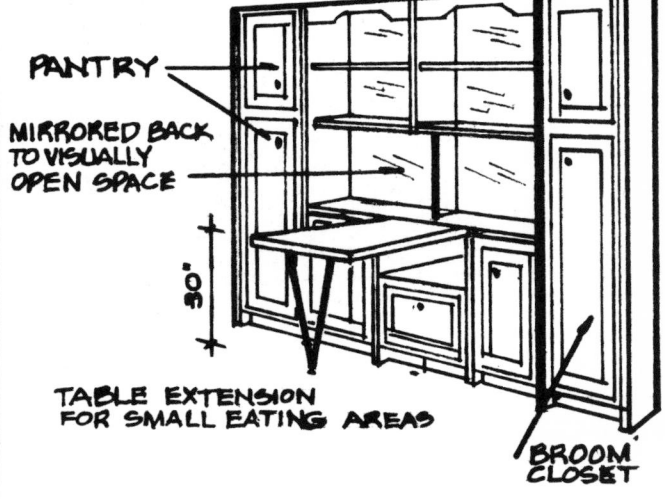

PANTRY

MIRRORED BACK
TO VISUALLY
OPEN SPACE

30"

TABLE EXTENSION
FOR SMALL EATING AREAS

BROOM
CLOSET

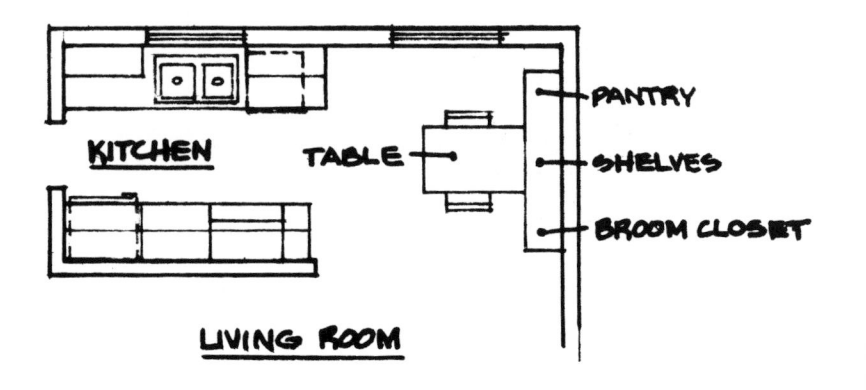

KITCHEN

TABLE

PANTRY

SHELVES

BROOM CLOSET

LIVING ROOM

NOTES

WIRE SHELVES CAN TURN A BLANK
WALL INTO FULL STORAGE OF A
VARIETY OF THINGS.

NOTES

STORAGE IN DINING AREAS
FREES SPACE IN KITCHEN
CABINETS FOR COOKWARE
STORAGE.

Courtesy: Charles Barone Co.

ABOVE:
CORNER CABINET ADDS
STORAGE & DECORATION.

RIGHT:
DECORATIVE & USEFUL
ARE THESE WALL-UNITS

NOTES

COMBINING COLLECTIBLES ON A WALL ADDS INTEREST TO THE ROOM & PROVIDES STORAGE FOR THEM

DOWELS FITTED INTO A WOOD PANEL ON EITHER SIDE OF THIS BAR HOLD FOOTED GLASSES & MUGS.

STORAGE UNITS

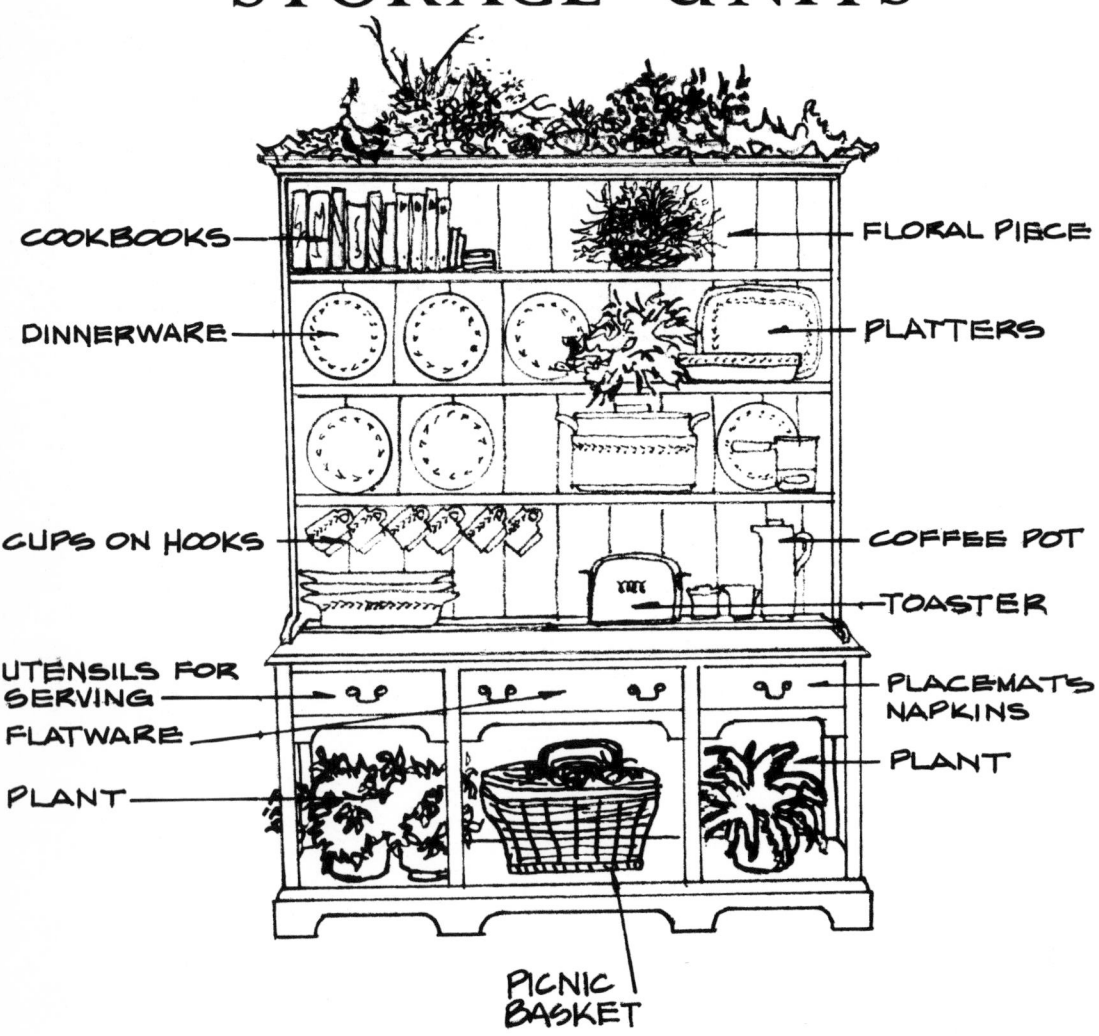

COOKBOOKS — FLORAL PIECE

DINNERWARE — PLATTERS

CUPS ON HOOKS — COFFEE POT

— TOASTER

UTENSILS FOR SERVING — PLACEMATS NAPKINS

FLATWARE —

PLANT — PLANT

PICNIC BASKET

A HUTCH OR BUFFET IN THE DINING AREA WILL FREE CABINET SPACE FOR OTHER STORAGE NEEDS.

NOTES

Courtesy: Armstrong Co.

WALL STORAGE IS DECORATIVE & FUNCTIONAL. MODULAR
CABINETS MAY BE USED & STACKED TOGETHER FOR A
VARIETY OF SPACE OPTIONS.

NOTES

A STURDY CART CAN SERVE MANY NEEDS; BRINGING
FOOD FROM THE CAR TO APARTMENT, EXTRA WORK
SPACE IN THE KITCHEN & A SERVING CART.
BE SURE ITS MADE WELL & IS ATTRACTIVE.

NOTES – LIGHTING

Courtesy: Mary Fisher Kitchens

UNDERCABINET LIGHTING FIXTURES SHOULD SHINE
LIGHT ON COUNTER TOP & NOT BE SEEN BELOW
THE CABINET. SELECT A FIXTURE THAT HAS AN
ELECTRICAL OUTLET & SWITCH ON THE UNIT.

NOTES

Courtesy: Lightolier Co.

NEW LIGHT STICKS FROM LIGHTOLIER CAN BE
ADDED AS NEEDED TO HELP CORRECT A
LIGHTING PROBLEM AT WORK AREAS.

USE & CARE GUIDE

USE & CARE GUIDE

KITCHEN UTENSILS & APPLIANCES

Most kitchen appliances (large and small) come with use and care guides prepared for your information by the manufacturers. Unfortunately, most of us do not take the time to read these little jewels and play it by ear until something goes wrong. It is my wish that you refer to this use and care guide for the basic and general information it offers, and refer to your manufacturer's guide for the specific utensils or appliance. The money you can save may be your own. Heavier gauge utensils hold their shape and provide more even heat distribution and are easier to clean than utensils warped because they are so light weight.

Courtesy: Mary Fisher Kitchens

KNIVES

Without good knives, you are greatly limited in your ability to perform many tasks in the kitchen. Buy the best knives, one or two at a time if you must, that your budget will allow. I can't imagine how many recipes have had just a touch of the cook's own "spice", red in color, added to a dish because he or she was cutting improperly with a dull knife or worse yet a serrated steak knife. Smiling? I know, I've been there, too. Believe me, there is no greater pleasure than preparing vegetables, fruits, and meats for dishes when the knife is sharp and the task becomes easy. Every set of knives should have a sharpening steel to keep it in good cutting condition. Be sure to purchase yours with the knives. Many stores, gourmet kitchen shops, and blade shops offer knife sharpening services. Good knives should never be used to open cans, bottles, cartons or cut paper. Always cut on wood, or wood chopping block. **DO NOT SOAK** your knives, no matter what they are made of. Good blades really shouldn't be put into the dishwasher either. While going to college, I worked in a butcher shop; never did either man ever throw his knives around, put them in water to soak, or cut hot food with them. When they were finished with the knife they were using, it was dipped in warm soapy water and immediately dried. They always cut on a large butcher block.

Carbon steel knives may discolor and stain. The best way to avoid this is to wipe them immediately after using them and then when you're finished with the job, wash and dry them. Acids will discolor carbon blades and should this happen, rub the blade with an emery cloth. (Emery cloth or paper can be obtained at any lumber yard or hardware store).

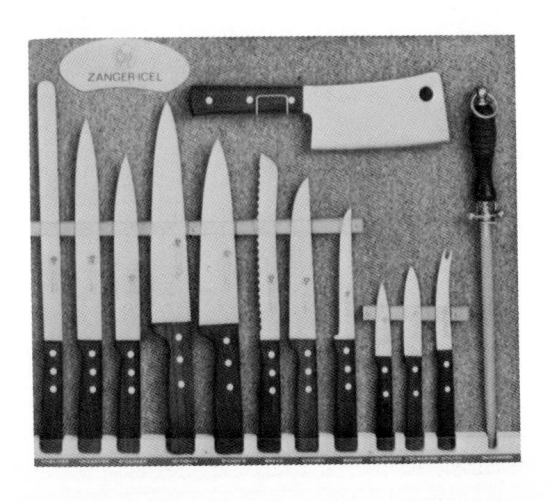

USE & CARE GUIDE (cont.)

GLASS, PORCELAIN ENAMEL, EARTHENWARE

Because many of us are cooking with microwaves today, glass and earthenware are cooking utensils we find ourselves using constantly. (With my microwave, I also use paper, plastic, crystal, and wood).

GLASS

Wash in soapy water and if food is stuck to the surface, soak in warm soapy water with a teaspoon or two of ammonia. Be sure to rinse thoroughly. If food still remains, use a fine steel-wool pad or plastic scrubbing pad.

PORCELAIN ENAMEL

Follow the manufacturer's instructions and use and care guide. Porcelain and enamel are the same term. It is a glass type material that has been fused to metal. If treated carelessly, it will chip. The porcelain interiors of self-cleaning ovens when going through the cleaning process are heated slowly and cooled slowly so that the materials making up the ovens are allowed to expand and contract at their own rate. This prevents cracking and crasing of the materials. This same principle applies to your porcelain cookware. When you have finished cooking in it, let it cool down before placing it in soapy water for washing. If food remains stuck to the finish, let it soak in soapy water with ammonia added to it for a while.

EARTHENWARE

This category includes all types of clayware, which can be quite porous. Following the use and care guides provided by the manufacturer will provide specific information for your particular cookware. Many clay products should be seasoned before using and some are designed to be soaked in water for a steaming effect when in the oven. Refer to the use and care guide. Generally, washing in soap and water is all that is necessary for cleaning.

PLASTIC UTENSILS

Plastic spoons, forks, tongs, spatulas, bowls and many other utensils are light weight, colorful additions to today's kitchens. Caring for them is easy. Simply wash in soapy water and dry. Do not use abrasive cleaners or pads on them, for they will scratch the finish and allow grease and dirt to collect. When cooking around heated areas (ovens, ranges, BBQ grills) be sure utensils are placed safely away from the heat source. This is also true in the dishwasher. Place your plastic items on the top rack of the dishwasher, not on the bottom near the heating element which dries the dishes. Plastic can be used in the microwave.

USE & CARE GUIDE (cont.)

WOOD UTENSILS

Salad bowls, unless they have been filled with fish, can be simply wiped out with a paper towel and stored in the open air. They will be fresh and ready to be used. When I have occasionally washed mine (through ignorance, I might add, and fear of germs) my bowls have become sticky. All woodenware should be kept away from open flames and protected from sitting on electric surface units of ranges or being placed on electric elements of the oven. When woodenware becomes split, cracked or very worn it should be thrown out. Because it is so porous, these utensils in poor condition are very unsanitary. Wood cutting boards should be made of hardwood (maple, cherry) and are generally finished with a very hard sealer. If this sealer has been cut into or scratched, it will be necessary to clean your cutting board with about 1 tablespoon of bleach to 1 quart of water. Pour it or sponge it over the cutting board and then rinse in very hot water from the faucet, and wipe with paper towels. Let the cutting board dry in the sun if possible.

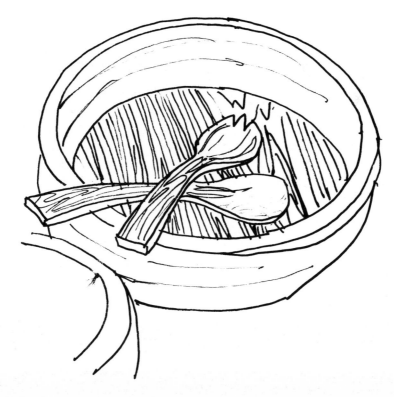

USE & CARE GUIDE (cont.)

METAL UTENSILS

Most metal utensils are very easy to care for; soap and water washing. However, if you are doing the dishes by hand, remember metal will show water spots if left to dry without a dish towel. For specific care of the various metals (copper, brass, etc.), see the section on that metal.

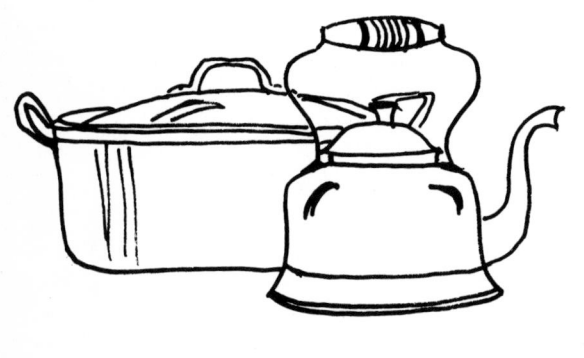

COPPER & BRASS

Never use a metal spoon or utensil in a lined copper pot, pan or other utensil. The lining is very delicate and could be mared or scraped off. Copper reacts to acids such as lemon juice, wine and vinegar causing unpleasant color and flavor. Be sure the copper you use is a heavy gauge and lined. Copper and brass with a lacquer coating must have that coating removed before cooking with it. To do so, fill a large container with water containing 1 tablespoon of washing soda per 1 quart of water and 1 more for good measure. Bring the water to a boil and place the piece (copper or brass) in the boiling water for 15 to 20 minutes. Remove the piece and the lacquer should peel right off. Acetone (available at drug stores) can replace the boiling water method if you like. The interior lining should never be cleaned with an abrasive or caustic cleaner. (Including scouring powders and steel wool). Remember your copper and brass pieces are delicate members of the kitchen and deserve your tender loving care. Copper and brass cleansers are available commercially, however, lemon juice or vinegar and salt will do quite well. Make a paste of lemon juice and salt or vinegar and salt and rub this mixture over the copper with a soft cloth, wash in hot sudsy water and rinse, then dry with a soft cloth. This method can be used on lined and unlined vessels. If the lining is wearing thin or has been scratched off, take the piece to an expert to be replated.

USE & CARE GUIDE (cont.)

NON-STICKING COATINGS

Wash in soapy water. Should something "stick" usually because you have used a sharp utensil and scratched the surface and the sticking is at that point, use a plastic scrubber pad or sponge. Then re-condition the pan with a light coating of oil.

STAINLESS STEEL

Washing your stainless steel in soapy water or the dishwater is quite satisfactory for most cleaning. However, if some food has stuck to the pot, or pan, cover the food with about ¼" of water and place it over medium heat on your range. When the water comes to a boil, turn heat down and let it simmer for about 5 minutes. Then turn the heat off and let the pan of water cool; stains should come off very easily. To wipe out the inside of the pan, use a soft dish cloth, paper towel, or plastic scrapper. Never use abrasives or wire pads on your stainless steel, they will remove some of the steel. I use a product called "Soft Scrub" which you can find in your supermarket. It's a mild abrasive, liquid cleanser which won't scratch the metal and adds a shine to the steel. I am very impressed with the product when using it on an old toaster and chrome on an old range; they really cleaned up beautifully.

USE & CARE GUIDE (cont.)

IRON WARE

My mother and grandmother cooked some of the most fabulous meals in cast iron cookware and as I recall Gramma was the one who taught me how to season a skillet and my Mom who suffered when I washed her favorite seasoned skillet and lid. Everyone should allow themselves to enjoy cooking in a skillet that has been seasoned.

HOW TO SEASON AN IRON PAN:

We used soapy water from Ivory soap. Don't use detergent. Rinse thoroughly and dry completely. Pour 1½ tablespoons of salad oil into the pan and spread it over all the surface with a paper towel. Now add enough oil to cover the bottom of the pan. Place it in a 325ºF to 350ºF oven until the oil is hot but not smoking. Carefully remove the pan and turn it so the oil covers the sides and bottom. Add just a little more oil and return it to an oven set at 200ºF. Let sit for about 1½ hours and then turn the oven off and let the pan stay there overnight. In the morning, remove the pan and drain the excess oil. Wipe it with paper towels and it's now ready to use. (When you've finished cooking in it, simply wipe it out with a soft cloth and warm water. Dry it with a soft cloth and it's ready to use again. Don't wash it with detergent or you'll have to re-season it. (For those of you who feel this is unsanitary I would like to say that my mother raised five of us with apparent success cooking with seasoned iron pans; my brothers are over six feet, six inches and very healthy athletes.)

Acid foods may cause a chemical reaction in iron pans and should be cooked in other types of cookware. (this includes wines).

USE & CARE GUIDE (cont.)

SILVER

Silver pieces stored in airtight chests, boxes or drawers and wrapped in anti-tarnish "Pacific" cloth will tarnish less than if left unprotected. Cleaning silver should be done as soon as possible after being used. **DO NOT SOAK.** Wash in warm water and add a few drops of ammonia to the water to cut grease and add shine to the silver.

Dry by hand immediately. Eggs contain sulphur which blackens silver. If silver is being used with egg dishes, or food containing raw egg, such as mayonnaise, be sure to wash immediately and use some silver polish, silver cloth, or good paste to remove tarnish and then follow with a warm sudsy bath. Dry with a soft cloth.

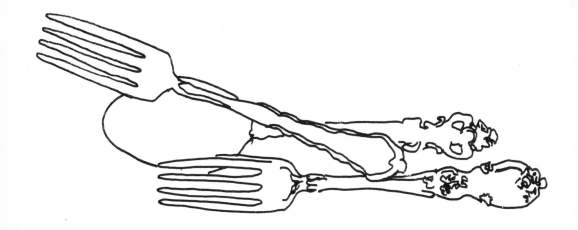

ALUMINUM

Aluminum that is heavy gauge is terrific to cook in. It conducts heat beautifully and is less likely to warp or dent than thinner aluminum pans. Alkalies and a few acids may pit the pans and in the case of alkalies, even discolor the aluminum. Not to worry. The discoloration will disappear when you cook some tomatoes in the utensil. Should you not care to cook the tomatoes, place the pan on the range and add vinegar and water and simmer for fifteen or twenty minutes. This reaction to some foods does not make cooking in aluminum harmful to your health and there are many well-known authorities who have so stated. (Gertrude Harris, author of POTS & PANS, etc.) Cleaning aluminum consists of using warm soapy water. Do not use harsh abrasives on your pots and pans nor metal scrub pads.

Courtesy:
Mary Fisher Kitchens

APPLIANCES

Major appliances such as range, ovens, refrigerators should have use and care guides available for your use. Follow them completely. If you are in an apartment or have moved to a house and the use and care guides are missing, take down the manufacturer's name and the model number of the appliance and contact the manufacturer requesting a guide to follow. Some basic principles to follow when cleaning your major appliances are as follows: Do not use abrasive cleansers on the various finishes. If you have a continuous clean oven, (Catalytic cleaning process) do not use any oven cleansers or detergents. This method of cleaning operates when heat of oven cooking causes the catalyst in the oven walls to activate. Any destruction of the catalyst by other chemicals or abrasive materials will cause the cleaning system to be ineffective. Because most microwave ovens cook without heat (some manufacturers have available models that allow you to cook with or without heat) cleaning them can be done with a soft dish cloth or sponge and warm soapy water.

Small appliances, i.e. toasters, coffee maker, food processor, mixer, etc., come with use and care guides which should also be followed. **Do not use** abrasive cleansers on your appliances. If you will just remember that the finish of all your appliances and utensils acts as skin to protect them, and should be cared for as you would care for your own skin, (gently, I hope) you will have useful tools to work with, not problems to contend with.

REMEMBER: FOLLOW THE MANUFACTURER'S USE AND CARE INSTRUCTIONS

RECOMMENDED BOOKS

Listed below are books with a great deal of information concerning kitchen organization and basic pots and pans "know-how".
Your local library offers a variety of information books along with selections of many cookbooks.

POTS & PANS
Gertrude Harris, 101 Productions, San Francisco. (A must book for your kitchen, especially if you are going to invest in quality tools.)

JOY OF COOKING
Erma S. Rombauer, Bobbs-Merrill Co. Indianapolis / N.Y. (This is the best cookbook for a beginner. It explains methods, techniques, and basic principles.)

THEORY & PRACTICE
OF GOOD COOKING
James Beard, Alfred K. Knopf, Inc., New York (You'll love this book and it's recipes for the basic information you receive, especially if you're into cooking.)

COOKERY FOR 1 or 2
Barbara Swain, H.P. Books Tucson, Arizona. (Designed to meet the needs of the couple or single person, this book has useful information and ·excellent recipes.)

KITCHEN REMODELING FILE

Mary Fisher Knott, Knott Communications, Alhambra, Ca. (This organizer guides you through a complete kitchen remodeling. Excellent on design and organization.